Bocardo Bramantip

The Abraham Lincoln Myth

Bocardo Bramantip

The Abraham Lincoln Myth

ISBN/EAN: 9783337183943

Printed in Europe, USA, Canada, Australia, Japan

Cover: Foto ©Andreas Hilbeck / pixelio.de

More available books at **www.hansebooks.com**

25 Cents

THE ABRAHAM LINCOLN MYTH

By BOCARDO BRAMANTIP

The MASCOT PUBLISHING CO.,

169 Sixth Avenue,

MASCOT LIBRARY, ISSUED MONTHLY { No. 6.—August 15, 1894. $3.00 per Year.

NEW YORK.

Entered at New York Post Office as Second-Class Matter.

THE ABRAHAM LINCOLN MYTH.

THE ABRAHAM LINCOLN MYTH

AN ESSAY IN "HIGHER CRITICISM"

BY

BOCARDO BRAMANTIP

*Huxleyan Professor of Dialectics in the University
of Congo*

FROM THE THIRTY-SEVENTH CENTURY MAGAZINE OF
APRIL, A. D. 3663

NEW YORK
THE MASCOT PUBLISHING CO.
1894

THE MERSHON COMPANY PRESS,

RAHWAY, N. J.

This anticipatory criticism is republished with a few emendations (conforming, however, to an authentic MS. of Bocardo Bramantip) from the *Catholic World* of November and December, 1893.

It is apparent that the variety of "Higher Criticism" upon which the African Critic has modeled his "Essay" is that practiced by controversialists of the Agnostic School.

THE
ABRAHAM LINCOLN MYTH.

———

LAST New Year's Day the Eigh-
teenth Centennial of the Emancipation
Proclamation of Abraham Lincoln was
celebrated with great *éclat.* Wherever
African civilization has extended,
through the four quarters of the globe,
the children of Africa, and the nations
they have civilized, celebrated the festi-
val with joy and enthusiasm. Never to
be forgotten was the spectacle on the
banks of the Victoria-Nyanza, at the
unveiling of the statue of " Lincoln Sign-

ing the Emancipation Proclamation "—
the masterpiece of the great Natalian
sculptor, Durango.

The president of the Universal Con-
federation of Nations presided in person
over the ceremonies, which were wit-
nessed by the assembled multitudes of
Africa's sons, and pilgrims of every race
and clime on the face of the earth.

It could not but impress all with the
thought that this is, in truth, an era of
good feeling and universal brotherhood.

Now, I have no disposition to cast a
shadow on the general rejoicing by the
expression of any disagreeable skepticism, and it is not altogether a pleas-
urable undertaking to dispel the happy
delusion under which my countrymen are

laboring in honoring an event which, as
I maintain, is not known ever to have
taken place. On the contrary, in a certain way, I, and all other advanced
thinkers, who look upon the popular
tradition of Abraham Lincoln and his
Emancipation Proclamation as a myth of
the Dark Ages, may consistently, not-
withstanding our want of faith, unite
with our African brethren in this jubilee,
precisely as the agnostics of the nineteenth century took part in the festivities
of Christmas. All we ask is to be
allowed to accept the tradition in a
rational way ; that is to say, as the con-
crete poetic or legendary expression of
great abstract underlying ideas—as, for
instance, that " Truth crushed to earth

shall rise again "—and the inherent power of the African race to attract to itself as to a magnet the moral forces of the universe, in the eternal struggle for the enfranchisement of the soul and the elevation of humanity.

But unfortunately a narrow and fanatical spirit seems to have taken possession of those who managed this latest Abraham Lincoln centennial. This spirit found very obnoxious expression by the orator of the day at the unveiling of the Lincoln statue, to which I have just alluded. He was no less a personage than the principal of the Law School of the University of Uganda.

He seized the opportunity to speak

in a censorious, not to say contempt-
uous tone, of those who do not accept
the popular story as "gospel truth,"
even going so far as to charge them
with juggling with history.

I feel entirely justified, under this
provocation, in speaking out my mind
freely on this matter.

I had not supposed that any man
who had a reputation for scholarship
to lose would venture, at this day, to
avow his belief in the Abraham Lincoln legend. But it seems I am mistaken. For the distinguished principal
of the Uganda Law School boldly
avows that he fully and firmly believes
in the literal truth of this extra-
ordinary story. Far be it from me to

rebuke his temerity. Indeed, I cannot forbear to express my profound admiration for the courage he thus displays in facing the ridicule of the advanced thinkers of this thirty-seventh century. Only when he makes the astounding assertion that this story is true beyond all reasonable doubt, and has been accepted as true by the best scholars of every age. since the nineteenth century, and proceeds to give a long list of historians who, as he asserts, express this belief, I feel called upon to warn the African public that they ought not to listen to this man.

It is galling to our pride to be told that our brethren in America were indebted for their freedom to a white man—one of the degenerate Caucasian race.

But what is to be expected of a lawyer when dealing with a question of evidence?

One might as soon be expected to listen patiently to a theologian venturing to enter the lists of controversy with a professional scientist upon a question of biblical history or criticism. He is to be distrusted from the outset.

We all know how vigorously and how effectively, in the nineteenth century, the Aristotle of our New Dialectics warned the British public not to pay any attention to theologians when disputing questions of biblical history and criticism with a professor of biology.

It is well known that the very chair which the principal of the Law School fills was endowed by a wealthy and credulous admirer of Abraham Lincoln —Marino Tobago—upon the express condition that every year, on Emancipation Day, its occupant should deliver a panegyric on the great American President and his services to the African race.

Is it not apparent, then, that here was a direct bribe to pervert history? For since it would be absurd to deliver a panegyric on a man who never lived, or to extol his services to the African race if he never rendered any service, the learned principal could not, of course, be expected to investigate the questions of Lincoln's existence and services with an unbiased mind, at the risk of reaching conclusions which would make it impossible for him, with any self-respect, to retain his place.

The learned principal of the Law School displays too much feeling for an historical critic. He manifests in his address a profound veneration for the martyred President. He evidently believes this story with his whole soul.

This alone disqualifies him from exercising a dispassionate and impartial judgment upon the questions at issue.

The scientist or the agnostic, on the other hand, never has any fixed belief, and is as ready to change his views for newer theories, as he is to change his clothes with the rise and fal' of the thermometer.

It is obvious, then, that he is incomparably better fitted to get at the truth of any historical question than a man who is handicapped by strong convictions. But let this pass.

I now propose to examine critically the popular tradition, upon the accepted principles of agnostic dialectics, as they have been transmitted to us from the great masters of the art in the nineteenth century.

What is the story we are asked to believe? Stripped of everything that is non-essential, reduced to what its advocates claim is the assured *residuum* after all controversy, it is, briefly stated, as follows:

About the year 1860, on the eve of the great Civil War in America, there suddenly appeared as a great public leader a man of obscure origin, named Abraham Lincoln.

Although previously wholly unknown to the great mass of the people, he was chosen President of the republic, and as the principles he represented were looked upon with abhorrence and fear by nearly one-half the nation, his election precipitated a rebellion. But he showed himself from the very outset to be a man of destiny—the greatest of statesmen and the wisest of rulers. During the

course of the war, and, as it is commonly
stated, on the first day of January, 1863,
he issued a Proclamation emancipating
the slaves everywhere throughout the
territory in possession of the rebels.
This was practically tantamount to universal emancipation.   Thus was the slavery of the African race in America abolished.   He suppressed the Rebellion and
saved his country.

Elected to the Presidency a second
time, shortly after his inauguration,
while attending the theater on a Good
Friday night, he was assassinated by an
actor who, after committing this horri-
ble crime, leaped upon the stage, exclaiming, " Sic semper tyrannis — the
South is avenged !"   But although the

theater was crowded with people warmly devoted to the President, his murderer was allowed to withdraw unmolested. From the moment of his assassination Abraham Lincoln was looked upon as a martyr, and by the African people in America as their "Moses," who had led them out of the Egypt of their bondage. Such is the popular tradition.

Now, I frankly admit, at the outset, that I see no sufficient reason to doubt that such a man as Abraham Lincoln lived in America in the nineteenth century, and that he was President of the United States during the Civil War.

This admission ought to be set down

by my readers to my credit ; proving, as it does, my extreme fairness and moderation. At the same time I guard myself against being supposed to affirm that Abraham Lincoln did ever actually exist, or was ever actually President of the United States. I say this much by way of forewarning, as it is possible the exigencies of this controversy may require me to withdraw the admission just made ; for there is, as is well known, a brilliant school of historical critics who more or less question the historical reality of Abraham Lincoln, and the genuineness of all the alleged contemporary and early accounts of his times.

But, excepting so far as I have now

admitted, I maintain that the popular story of Abraham Lincoln is unhistoric —fit only to be relegated to the category of myths.

There is no good reason to think that he was ever re-elected to the Presidency, for we have no certain record of any official act of his subsequent to the close of his term of four years. He seems to have been succeeded immediately at the close of such term by one Andrew Johnson.

The story of his assassination suggests, in all its details, the hand of a novelist or a playwright. The time chosen for the tragedy, a Good Friday night; the place, a crowded theater; the assassin, a professional actor of tragedy; the

murderer's dramatic leap upon the
stage, brandishing the weapon of death
and exclaiming in dramatic tones, "Sic
semper tyrannis !" (which, it may be
remarked, was simply the legend of
the State of Virginia); the vast audi-
ence paralyzed with amazement or fear
—all these accessories seem like skill-
fully arranged settings for the tragic
climax of a romance or a drama. All
I here claim, however, is that the story
looks artificial and suspicious on its
face.

It is wholly immaterial that the story
appears to have been generally believed
by the American people in the latter
part of the nineteenth century, or in the
following three or four centuries; such

ancient belief does not even tend to prove that the story is true—it is rather a reason for doubting it. It is essential for the higher historical criticism— the *sine qua non* of its possibility—that the speculations of modern critics should not be handicapped by the beliefs of the people, or by the views of the so-called historians of early ages—before the dawn of Scientific Historical Criticism. For whatever any believer in this myth may say to the contrary, it is simply a fact that history—I mean true scientific history— had its origin with the African Renaissance. All that transpired before the overthrow of Aryan power in Europe and America, and the final triumph of

African supremacy in both hemispheres, belongs to the Dark Ages.

I know the Law School principal, like most others of his cloth, professes to take a totally different view of this matter. In order to be perfectly fair, I give what he has to say on this sub-. ject in his address in his own words, as follows :

"Conceding that posterity is better qualified than contemporaries to. form a just estimate of the character of public men and measures, and to discover through the development of institutions, whether civil or religious, the nature and inherent power of their germs, yet questions as to the *existence* of alleged historical facts are a wholly different matter. The general belief of the American people living, say, in the year 1894, and subsequently in that century, or in the centuries immediately following, in the popular story of Abraham Lincoln's life and death, and in the fact of the Emancipation Proclamation, and that such narratives as Horace Greeley's 'American Conflict' and General Grant's 'Personal Memoirs,' and the autobiographies of General Sherman and General Sheridan were authentic and credible, ought to be received as settling these questions for all time.

" The contemporaries of Lincoln, or those living in the times immediately

following, were vastly better qualified
to pass upon these matters than scholars
living in our own day; and while in
the lapse of time the evidence upon
which they acted must, in the nature
of things, have become to a great
extent lost or impaired, its import is
crystallized and preserved for all time
in the verdict of contemporaneous
and early common belief. Upon the
same principle, in the interpretation
of ancient documents, the wisdom of
centuries finds its expression in the
maxim of the common law—*Contempo-
ranea expositio est optima et fortis-
sima in lege.*

"These questions ought to be
treated, then, as *res judicata.* It is

about as irrational to refuse thus to accept the verdict of Lincoln's contemporaries, and of those who lived in early times succeeding him, and to insist on rewriting his history *de novo*, after the lapse of eighteen centuries, as it would be to insist on settling the question of the source of the Nile by making observations at its mouth, and refusing to credit the report of those who had looked upon its head-waters. Nor can it be doubted that the generations immediately succeeding received and retained the general belief of Lincoln's contemporaries on those matters in its essential integrity, and transmitted it in their turn to those who came after them.

"It is inconceivable that in the twentieth or succeeding centuries the original tradition should have become obliterated, or a new belief imposed upon mankind.

"Shakespeare thus illustrates the persistency and integrity of even oral tradition, in a dialogue between the young Prince Edward and the Duke of Buckingham on their way to the tower of London :

"'*Prince.* I do not like the Tower, of any place.

Did Julius Cæsar build that place, my lord ?

"'*Buckingham.* He did, my gracious lord, begin that place ;

Which, since, succeeding ages have
    re-edified. '

   "*'Prince.* Is it upon record, or else
    reported
Successively from age to age, he built
    it ?

   "*'Buckingham.* Upon record, my
    gracious lord.

   "*'Prince.* But say, my lord, it were
    not register'd,
Methinks the truth should live from
    age to age,
As 'twere retail'd to all posterity,
Even to the general all-ending day.' *

   "If this be true of purely oral tradition, and true as to a matter of com-

---

   * " Richard III.," act iii. scene 1.

paratively little importance, what like-
lihood is there that the contemporary
record of events of such vast import as
those we are now considering was lost
or falsified ?

" To believe this to have occurred is
to yield, at one and the same time, to
the extreme of credulity and the extreme
of skepticism. But these extremes
naturally meet together."

Thus far the learned principal of the
Law School.

Now, I submit that his notions are
wholly effete and untenable. Had they
prevailed, neither the Tübingen school in
the nineteenth century, nor the Timbuctoo school in the thirty-seventh, with

all their brilliant and varied theories, would have had a *raison d'être.*

It would have followed, for instance, that the results reached by Origen in the third century, Eusebius in the fourth, and St. Jerome in the fifth, all in substantial accord in settling the authenticity and text of the New Testament, would never have been superseded by the speculations of Strauss or Baur or Renan.

It is true that Origen, Eusebius, and St. Jerome were men of profound scholarship (I mean, of course, for their age), and unquestionably had the advantage of vastly more material, in the way of early manuscripts (since lost), than the critics of the nineteenth century.

But the latter made up for this disadvantage by the vast increase of the "historical temper," upon which our agnostic forefathers of the nineteenth century so well insisted.

While in the lapse of time early manuscripts disappeared, their place was more than supplied by the "imaginative" element, which, as a great authority, Mrs. Humphrey Ward says, is essential for the higher criticism. In her "New Reformation" she tersely describes the advanced school of higher criticism as "half scientific, half imaginative." *

Of these two elements it is obvious the "imaginative" is by far the most important, and has chiefly contributed

* *Nineteenth Century*, March, 1889, p. 457.

to the brilliant results in biblical criticism to which this school has mainly
devoted its attention.

I insist upon the opposite of my opponent's thesis, and maintain that critics of
the thirty-seventh century are better
qualified to pass upon the truth of the
popular story of Abraham Lincoln, and
the authenticity, competency, and credi-
bility of such narratives as Greeley's
" American Conflict " and Grant's " Personal Memoirs," than were those living
in the twentieth or in the latter part of
the nineteenth century.

The beliefs of the first century were
ignored by the critics of the nineteenth
as superstitious and incredible. The
scholarship of the nineteenth century

seems to us childish, crude, and inadequate. A thousand years hence the best results of modern criticism will doubtless be looked upon as mere literary curiosities, void of intrinsic value. And thus it must ever go on with the advance of thought (or of time) to the end. With each succeeding age the work must be done over again, and history must be rewritten or "reconceived" (as Mrs. Ward puts it), in the light of modern ideas. It follows from this discussion that in dealing with the Lincoln legend we should start with a *tabula rasa*, disregarding the beliefs and the so-called histories of early times, and proceed to reconstruct or "reconceive" the tradition, so as to conform it to the advanced views of modern critics.

The story is the outgrowth of "hero worship," so prevalent in the nineteenth century. The Aryan race was given to the love of the wonderful, and to the idolatry of its great men. We have this story of Lincoln, just as we have the stories of Columbus, of Washington, of Cromwell, of Charlemagne, of King Arthur, of Robin Hood, of Romulus and Remus, of the Cid, of Amadis de Gaul, and of Don Quixote. They are one and all the outgrowth of this love of the wonderful and of this "hero worship," and as Huxley said of miracles, I may with equal appositeness say of these stories: "If one is false all may be false."*

The age lacked "the historical temper." It was prone to believe every marvelous story told of its heroes. We have learned to expect such stories in the narratives of that time, but they are no longer acceptable to the dispassionate criticism of an age of scientific thought.

As was said by Mrs. Ward (in her "New Reformation") of historians before her time, we may now say of the historians of the nineteenth century: "They represented the exceptional, the traditional, the miraculous,

---

* "Essays Upon Some Controverted Questions" (1893), p. 374.

and they have had to give way to
the school representing the normal, the
historical, the rational." *

I reject this story, then, because it
is not only "traditional," but also
because, as viewed in the light of the
present day, it is "exceptional."

Precisely formulated, the postulate,
or first principle, upon which I reject
this tradition as a myth is as follows :
It is improbable and incredible that
such a career as that which the tradition ascribes to Abraham Lincoln
should occur in the thirty-seventh century; and if so, it is improbable and
incredible that it occurred in the nineteenth century. By a similar postu-

* *Nineteenth Century*, March, 1889, p. 467.

late, or first principle, our agnostic
predecessors in the nineteenth century
made short work of the Gospels. The
writers of the Gospels reported the
" miraculous." And as miracles since
the apostles were assumed to be
improbable and incredible, there was
no good reason why they should be
thought probable and credible in the
apostles' time.

The agnostic controversialist of the
nineteenth century did not assert, indeed, with Hume, as an *a priori* principle, that miracles were impossible, or
not, theoretically, susceptible of proof.
On the contrary, he did not admit any
such thing as an *a priori* principle at
all.

He merely said, like the Dutch jus-
tice of the peace : " I will consider the
evidence, and in four days I will de-
cide the case in favor of the plaintiff."

Possibly, however, my opponent
may deny my first principle, and
maintain that such a career as Lincoln's
is *not* incredible, and that it might be,
or even that it has been, paralleled in
modern times.

Well, there were those in the nineteenth century who denied the first
principle upon which our agnostic forefathers based their assault upon the
Gospels. These people denied that
miracles were incredible, either in the
time of the apostles or since their time,
and affirmed, on the contrary, "that

the Supreme Being has wrought miracles on earth ever since the time of the apostles," as well as in and before their time.

This struck at the root of the entire argument against the Gospel narratives, and it would be necessary, as against people who thus argued, to prove that miracles were incredible at any time. But those who thus objected were either Romanists or no better than Romanists, and of course it would have been a waste of time for a scientist or an agnostic to attempt to reason with people of that class.

If, however, my opponent requires me to demonstrate my first principle, to wit, that the reported career of Abra-

ham Lincoln is "exceptional" and incredible, viewed in the light of the
thirty-seventh century, I will proceed
at once to do so.

1. It remains to be proved that there
has been any career at all analogous to
that ascribed by the popular tradition
to Abraham Lincoln, or as "exceptional" as his, since the nineteenth
century, and especially in our own
day.

All I can say is it will be a difficult
job to satisfy an agnostic on this
point. Indeed, any proof offered may
be at once rejected as being testimony
to the "exceptional."

2. "Hero worship" is unknown to
modern civilization.

Individualism is looked upon as the bane of equality and a menace to the social equilibrium. Ever since the African Renaissance it has been the business of the state to educate the people, up and down, to a common level.

The same schools for all—the same school books, the same code of morals and manners carefully prescribed by the legislature, the same rules for dress and for the daily routine of occupation, including the same physical exercises, together with a careful adjustment of marriages under state supervision, and a careful selection of offspring fit to survive — all this has secured the complete equality of the

people, mentally, morally, and physi-
cally.

It is true · that a great thinker of the
nineteenth century, John Stuart Mill,
protested against this grand system of
governmental education, stigmatizing
it as "a mere contrivance for molding
people to be exactly like one another." *

Precisely. And it is a matter of con-
gratulation that Mill's protest was un-
heeded. The very thing he depre-
cated was the thing aimed at, *i. e.*,
"molding people to be exactly like one
another," and the elimination of "in-
dividuality of character and diversity in
opinions and mode of conduct." With
such success has the leveling process

---

* Mill on "Liberty," American edition, 1863, p. 205.

been carried out, that no citizen is in any respect the superior or the inferior of any other citizen. Neither we nor our fathers have ever known any other state of things.

" Hero worship," a thing impossible at the present day, is known to us only through the legends of former ages.

It follows from all this that the story of Abraham Lincoln, being improbable and incredible in the light of the present day, must be rejected as a myth of the Dark Ages. *Q. E. D.*

As the immediate occasion for this discussion was the alleged Emancipation Proclamation, it is proper I should give especial attention to the question of its authenticity.

But if I succeed in discrediting that supposititious document, I discredit at the same time the entire popular tradition of which it is a component part—for *falsum in uno, falsum in omnibus.*

I submit, then, the following six reasons for doubting the historic truth of the alleged Emancipation Proclamation.

I.

The first reason is based on the present state of the oldest record evidence. It will not be claimed, I suppose, that there is now extant any book or other document of the nineteenth century purporting to be a narrative of the fact in question. Every presumption is against the preservation of any such document, and its existence cannot be proved.

In the nineteenth century no original manuscript of the first age of the Christian era, or of the preceding two centuries, was known to be in existence.

The oldest manuscript of a date since the beginning of the Christian era was supposed to be the palimpsest of "Cicero de Republica" of the second century.

The oldest copies of Terence and of Sallust were of the fourth or fifth century.

The celebrated "Medicean Vergil" was also of the fourth or fifth century.

The oldest manuscript of the New Testament, the "Codex Vaticanus," was, as we learn from the article on "Palæography" in the "Encyclopædia Britannica," of the fourth century.

There was in these cases an hiatus of from three to six centuries between the writers and the oldest extant copies of their writings.

Now, as there is no good reason why history should not repeat itself in this respect, it was to be presumed that no copy or reprint of any publication of the nineteenth century would be found in this the thirty-seventh century older than from the twenty-third to the twenty-sixth century.

Indeed, a far greater hiatus was to be expected between the writers of the nineteenth century and the oldest copy of their writings, in the thirty-seventh, than between writers of the first and the oldest copy of their writings, in the nineteenth century. For before the discovery of the art of printing, the difficulty of making copies caused it to be a matter of far greater importance than afterward, to carefully preserve these copies. More durable material (parch-ment) was used, and copies were kept with the greatest care in monasteries, under the supervision of learned com-munities—the Benedictines and others, who devoted especial attention to the preservation of the sacred books, as well as of the great masterpieces of Grecian and Latin history and poetry and philosophy. With the invention of printing the ease and rapidity with which copies could be reproduced, and the perishable material used (paper), ren-dered the long preservation of first edi-tions a matter of little or no importance, and practically impossible.

Deposits in public libraries were no

guarantee of long preservation—*i. e.,*
for many centuries, The libraries of
the British Museum and of the American Congress were as liable to destruction by fire or mob as was the Alexan-
drian library, the largest of the ancient
world. The overthrow of the Roman
Empire, history tells us, involved in its
fate the destruction or dispersion of all
the great libraries of the empire.

But the canker of time would inevitably obliterate printed books, even if
they escaped the fury of fire and mob.*

---

* An interesting illustration of the perishableness of
original documents is the fate of the Declaration of Independence within a little over a century from its date.
The following is taken from the New York *Times* of
February 13, 1894 :

" WASHINGTON, February 12.—To-day the original

The people of the nineteenth century feared the destruction of their printed records, and sometimes attempted to avert or delay this fate by deposits in corner-stones. But where has there been found amid the ruins of New York or Washington or London any

copy of the Declaration of Independence was withdrawn from public exhibition in the State Department library, made into a roll, and placed in a tin box for filing with the archives of the Government. The rapid fading of the text of the declaration and the deterioration of the parchment on which it is engrossed, from exposure to the light and on account of age, rendered it impracticable for the department to allow it to be exhibited or handled longer. In lieu of the original document, a fac-simile will be placed on exhibition.

"Some years ago it was noticed that the ink on the original parchment was fading, and it has been gradually growing fainter. Recently chemists were called on to examine it, and they gave the opinion that the full strength

record of the Emancipation Proclamation which it can be demonstrated dates
back to the nineteenth century?

What conclusion is to be drawn from
all this?

Obviously, that in the hiatus between
the original records of the nineteenth
century and the oldest extant copies of
them—an hiatus of, from three to six
centuries, at least—the opportunity for
fraud and mistake was so great as to

---

of the ink could be brought out again by coating it with
a chemical solution. But this experiment was not tried,
owing to the fear that the precious paper might be in-
jured in some way, and also because no alteration could
be made, and nothing whatever done to it, without the
authority of an act of Congress. It required an act of
Congress to bring the declaration from Philadelphia to
Washington."

render these copies wholly untrust-
worthy.

It was in view of a similar hiatus
that Professor Huxley declared that, in
such an interval, "there is no telling
what additions and alterations and
interpolations may have been made." *

* Huxley's " Essays," p. 265.

II.

There can be no question that the early narratives of the Emancipation Proclamation, those purporting to be contemporaneous with this alleged event, as well as those written near the close of the nineteenth century and the following centuries, are all based on the same *groundwork.*

And of "the originator or originators of this groundwork" we know "absolutely nothing."

This proposition is susceptible of the clearest and most convincing proof. For what *was* this "groundwork"?

Beyond all controversy it was, mainly,

the *newspaper accounts* of the day; and
these newspaper accounts, it will not be
disputed, were *anonymous.*

Even the alleged contemporary
writers of formal history do not pre-
tend to have had any personal knowl-
edge of the proclamation, nor even to
have derived their information from eye-
witnesses. They undoubtedly obtained
their information from this original
"groundwork," and based their histories
on these *anonymous* reports. It follows
from this that no dependence can be
placed upon a "superstructure" built
upon a "groundwork" of whose originators we know "absolutely nothing." *

* Compare Huxley on the "groundwork" of the Syn-
optic Gospels, "Essays," p. 265.

III.

The story is wholly irreconcilable with
the Constitution of the United States.
Modern research has at last disentangled
the knotty problem of the organization
of the Ancient American Republic. It
was a complicated structure of States
within a state ; of powers distributed
between a general government and State
governments. But it is now agreed by
all scholars that the United States were
a government of *limited* powers, specifi-
cally defined by a written Constitution,
and that all powers not expressly or by
necessary implication vested in the gen-

eral government were reserved to the States and to the people.

The tenth article of the Constitution provides as follows :

" The powers not delegated to the United States by the Constitution, nor prohibited by it to the States, are re-served to the States respectively, or to the people."

Fortunately this Constitution, as might have been expected, has come down to our time intact. It is, probably, the best authenticated document of Ancient American literature. Now, there cannot be found anywhere in the Constitution any authority conferred on the President to abolish slavery. And as he could not obtain such authority

from any other source, it is clear he had
no power to issue an Emancipation
Proclamation.

The President had taken, as was
required of him, an oath to support this
Constitution. He is believed to have
been, above all things, an *honest* man,
and it is inconceivable that he violated
his oath.

It adds greatly to the force of this
argument that Lincoln himself, less than
four months before this alleged proclamation (of January 1, 1863), when
urged to issue an edict abolishing
slavery, replied that his object was to
save the Union "under the Constitution," showing clearly his determina-
tion not to violate the Constitution,

even for the purpose of saving the Union.

We learn from Greeley's " American Conflict," that as late as August 22, 1862, the President used the following language, in a letter written to Greeley himself :

" My paramount object is to save the Union, and not either to save or destroy slavery."

And again :

" As to the policy I would seem to be pursuing, as you say, I have not meant to leave anyone in doubt. I would save the Union ; I would save it in the shortest way *under the Constitution*" (vol. ii. p. 250). The italics are mine.

A deputation of Protestant clergy-

men from Chicago visited the President,
September 13, 1862, to urge him to
issue such a proclamation. But he
argued with them at length against
such a proceeding, saying, among other
things, that such a proclamation would
be as idle as "a pope's bull against the
comet" (*Id.*, p. 251).

There is not a scintilla of evidence
presented by Greeley to show that any
new light ever dawned upon the President's mind.

Now, it is true that in the oldest
copy we have of Greeley's book—which
must have been printed, as I have
already shown, several centuries after
Greeley's death—the alleged proclamation is inserted right on the heels of the

letter from which I have just quoted,
and of his interview with the Chicago
clergymen. And the following is the
only explanation that is given for its
abrupt appearance.

After speaking of the President's
reply to the deputation, which is men-
tioned above, the narrative is made to
say :

" The deputation had scarcely re-
turned to Chicago, and reported to
their constituents, when the great body
of the President's supporters were elec-
trified, while his opponents in general
were only still further alienated, by the
unheralded appearance of the following
proclamation," to wit : a proclamation
of September 22, 1862, announcing his

intention to issue the final Emancipation Proclamation on the first day of January, 1863 (*Id.*, p. 252).

Now, what sort of an explanation is this? Will it satisfy any rational Historical Critic? What reason does it assign for this "unheralded" and abrupt change of front? None whatever.

Abraham Lincoln is reputed to have been a man of remarkably clear and strong convictions, and of great tenacity of purpose. But to credit this remarkable and sudden change, is it not to make him out vacillating and "infirm of purpose"?

This is incredible. It is altogether more probable that he continued to maintain the position taken by him as late as September 13, 1862, and that the proclamations appearing in our copies of Greeley's book are interpolations of a later age. Everything indicates this. They are too abrupt, and are out of place in the narrative—out of harmony with the context.

IV.

The argument just presented may be characterized as an *a priori* reason, based upon the absence of constitutional authority, and the improbability that Lincoln transcended his constitutional powers.

The Thirteenth Amendment of the Constitution supplements this with an *a posteriori* reason for discrediting the story. By this amendment slavery was abolished. The amendment was adopted by Congress, and ratified by the States, in the year 1865.

Now, if slavery had already been abolished, by the Emancipation Proclamation, on the 1st of January, 1863, what is the meaning of this solemn farce of the Thirteenth Amendment ?

This amendment was adopted by a Congress composed almost entirely of the devoted political and personal friends of the President. And yet they do not so much as *allude* to his alleged great "Proclamation of Freedom," even by way of preamble. The amendment does not purport to *ratify* his act, but to be an original enactment.

This seems very strange.

· It puts the advocates of the proclamation in this dilemma : They must either admit that the Congress of 1865 knew nothing of this alleged document, or considered it of no value. But it may be said that Lincoln's proclamation only freed the slaves within the Confederate lines, while the amendment enfranchised them everywhere throughout the United States. But this is a very poor quibble. Everyone knows that all but a very small fraction of the slaves were within the Confederate lines, and that if slavery were abolished throughout the Con- federacy, it could not survive a single year on the borders of the free States. So that if it had been abolished, by the proclamation, in the Confederate States in 1863, it would have ceased to exist anywhere in the United States before 1865, and there would have been no reason for the Thirteenth Amendment, and nothing for it to operate upon.

V.

I come now to an* argument to which I attach the greatest importance, and which anyone familiar with agnostic dialectics must see is fatal to the claim that Abraham Lincoln promulgated the Emancipation Proclamation.

This argument may be termed the argument from *silence*.

It will be conceded, of course, that none of the alleged comtemporary narratives of the Civil War is entitled to greater credit for authenticity, competency, and truthfulness than the "Personal Memoirs of U. S. Grant."

He was, himself, not only the most conspicuous chieftain of the war, but was also afterward President of the Republic for two consecutive terms. His personal relations with Lincoln were of the closest nature. The "Memoirs" were carefully prepared by him toward the close of his life, and were published about the year 1885, less than a quarter of a century after Lincoln's death.

They were looked upon by the American people as a perfectly trustworthy narrative, written by the most competent of narrators.

Now, there is not to be found anywhere in the two good-sized volumes of these Memoirs so much as a single

mention of any Emancipation Proclamation! What is to be thought of this?
The inference is inevitable, that General Grant had never heard of any
such document.

It is idle to suggest that this matter
lay outside the scope of Grant's book.
His work is very comprehensive and
complete. It deals not only with his
own campaigns, but with those of Sherman and the other great generals of
the war. It deals also with the political history of the war, including, of
course, the slavery question, which
was the cause of the war.

Moreover, emancipation, had it taken
place as alleged, must inevitably have
proved an extremely important factor,

as a "war measure," in the campaigns in which Grant was engaged and of which he was writing.

It is inconceivable that he would make no allusion to this great culminating act in the "irrepressible conflict," to this Magna Charta of the African race in the United States, if any such proclamation had been issued.

The significance of his silence can scarcely be overestimated.

For a similar reason Professor Huxley argued that the "Sermon on the Mount" is not genuine, because Mark does not give it—although Matthew and Luke do.*

If "logic is logic," judgment must

* "Essays," pp. 324-325.

go against the proclamation, upon the "argument from silence."

If, now, it be asked why I insist that Grant's "Memoirs" are the most authentic and most credible of all the contemporaneous narratives of the Civil War, and why I refuse to give credence to other narratives which *do* purport to give an account of the Emancipation Proclamation, it is a sufficient answer to say that Grant's "Memoirs" *conform* to what I conceive to be the truth of history respecting the matter now in question, and that the other narratives do not. I give the preference to the "Memoirs" for the same reason that Professor Huxley appears to have given the preference to St. Mark's Gospel. It best conformed, he thought, to the view he was advocating of the Crucifixion, and what " happened after the Crucifixion."*

In its brevity of narrative it omits some statements contained in the other Gospels, which would, if accepted, have made it impossible for him to stick to his theory.

Indeed, we find a great diversity among the advanced critics of the nineteenth century in the matter of preference. Some of them preferred Matthew, others Luke, and others again John.

Renan appears to have varied in his preferences.

My readers will pardon me, I trust,

* *Id.,* p. 328.

for citing here Mrs. Ward's picturesque
summary of the results of German criticism toward the close of the nineteenth
century :

"And what is the whole history of
German criticism but a history of
brilliant failures, from Strauss down-
ward ?

" One theorist follows another—now
Mark is uppermost as the *Ur-Evangelist*,
now Matthew ; now the synoptics are
sacrificed to St. John, now St. John to
the synoptics. Baur relegates one after
another of the epistles to the second
century because his theory cannot do
with them in the first.

" Harnack tells you that Baur's theory

is all wrong, and that Thessalonians and Philippians must go back again. Volkmar sweeps together Gospels and Epistles in a heap toward the middle of the second century as the earliest date for almost all of them ; and Dr. Abbot, who, as we are told, has absorbed all the learning of all the Germans, puts Mark before 70 A. D., Matthew just before 70 A. D., and Luke about 80 A. D.

"Strauss' mythical theory is dead and buried by common consent. Baur's tendency theory is much the same ; Renan will have none of the Tübingen school ; Volkmar is already antiquated, and Pfleiderer's fancies are now in the order of the day."*

* *Nineteenth Century*, March, 1889, p. 462.

This may at first sight suggest an intellectual Donnybrook Fair. But to one possessing "the historical temper" there is discernible in the midst of all this apparent confusion the constant struggle for *conformity to theory.* This is the theme which brings harmony out of what *otherwise* seems hopeless discord.

In the first place the theory accredits the record, and then the record proves the theory.

Grant's "Memoirs" conforming to my theory, I give them the preference over all other narratives. And his "Memoirs" bear out my theory.

VI.

There is another argument suggested
by Grant's " Memoir's," or perhaps it
would be more accurate to say another
way of putting the same argument—
to wit, the *discrepancies* in the narratives.

This was a fruitful source of objection to the Gospels by our agnostic
forefathers in the nineteenth century.

Thus Professor Huxley, in objecting
to the story of demoniacal possession in
the Gadarene country, or, as he play-
fully calls it, " the Gadarene pig af-

fair," dwells on the fact that Mark and Luke mention but one possessed man, while Matthew mentions two.* Of course the inference is obvious—there was no such " affair." Unfortunately I do not have at hand any of the histories of the American Civil War written subsequent to the year 1894, or I would be able, I think, to make out a pretty formidable list of just such discrepancies.

But the one I have just been considering, between Grant's " Memoirs," and the other alleged contemporary narratives, for instance, Greeley's " American Conflict," is sufficient for the purpose of the argument.

* "Essays," p. 346.

Attention has already been called to the fact that all these narratives, so far from being independent authorities, are all based on one original "groundwork." The "groundwork" has disappeared in the lapse of time. The strength of the "superstructure"—*i. e.*, the narratives based on it—depends, of course, on their fidelity to or conformity with the "groundwork." Now, there is no way by which this conformity can be known to exist excepting by the agreement of these narratives with each other. Here we have the key by which to distinguish the original story from the glosses and interpolations of later times.

In there spects in which they all agree

we may, in the absence, of course, of
some other objection, concede that they
reproduce the original story. But as to
all matters in which they disagree with
each other, all the narratives are to be
rejected. For how are we to account
for the discrepancies? And which
statement is to be received as true,
and which rejected as false? Truth
is always consistent with itself; and
when two witnesses tell different stories
one of them must be untruthful or
mistaken.

The *discrepancy*, then, between Grant
and Greeley as to the matter now in
question—Greeley purporting to give the
proclamation, and Grant making no mention of it—warrants me in concluding

that the story of the proclamation was no part of the original "groundwork" upon which both their narratives are built, and that it should therefore be rejected as spurious.

It is singular how obtuse the Principal of the Law School, and, as for that matter, lawyers in general are, to the force of this argument from discrepancy.

They seem to make nothing of discrepancies in the details of a story, and to expect them even from witnesses whom they regard as honest, unbiased, and intelligent.

The ordinary legal view is thus stated by Starkie in his " Law of Evidence ":

" It has been well remarked by a great observer, that 'the usual character of human testimony is substantial truth under circumstantial variety.' It so rarely happens that witnesses of the same transaction perfectly and entirely agree in all points connected with it that an entire and complete coincidence in every particular, so far from strengthening their credit, not unfrequently engenders a suspicion of practice and concert " (vol. i. p. 468).

Having occasion to visit one of our courts the other day, I chanced to find an accident case on trial.

A boy, some ten years old, running across the street, had been knocked down and killed by the horses drawing some vehicle.   The witnesses of the occurrence, all of them, apparently, people of ordinary intelligence, and wholly disinterested, differed very widely in many of the circumstances.   One of them said the boy was running from the north to the south side of the street.   Another said he was running from the south to the north side.   One saw only one boy running. Another saw *two* boys, one chasing the other.

Now, in a mind properly indoctrinated with the methods of agnostic dialectics, these discrepancies would raise a doubt as to whether there was any boy running at all—or any accident.   But, strange to say, neither lawyers, judge, nor jury seemed to have any trouble on these points.

It is fortunate for the "higher historical criticism" that it knows nothing of legal rules of evidence.

VII.

What, then, is the real explanation of the story of the Emancipation Proclamation?

The earliest theory since the era of higher criticism was that of Dr. Dokamok, to wit : that the story was purely allegorical, having as its substratum of truth the triumph of liberty in its "irrepressible conflict" with slavery. But the rising Timbuctoo school considered that Dokamok had gone too far in his destructive criticism, and recoiled from it.

He himself, after his beard had grown,

practically abandoned this theory of his nursery days.

The theory which immediately super-seded the allegorical was that of the famous Professor Felapton. He was probably the first entomologist of his age. His great work on the "Mos-quito" is a marvel of patient research. No one could be better equipped, then, for historical investigation. He un-earthed the fact that in the American Republic there were two great parties differing, *toto cœlo*, in their interpretation of the Constitution, to wit: the strict constructionists and the liberal construc-tionists; and that after the close of the Civil War, which turned the tide toward liberalism, the advocates of liberal construction pressed their advantage with great persistency and fertility of resource. It was under the influence of this liberal tendency that the story had its origin and its growth.

Upon the slender foundation of the few historic facts conceded at the outset of this article, there was gradually built up, under the influence of this tendency, the story which has come down to our times—as the tradition of an actual occurrence.

Nothing could be more effectively cited as a precedent to extend the power of the chief magistrate beyond the letter of the Constitution, when it became important to invoke the extreme exercise of executive power.

But the view which now obtains nearly universal acceptance among advanced thinkers is the latest theory of the new Timbuctoo school—to wit: that the alleged proclamation is a forgery of the twentieth century.

There is no doubt that some time in the course of the twentieth century, in a very exciting contest for the Presidency, one of the candidates bore the name of Lincoln. His given name is not certainly known, nor is it entirely clear whether or not he was a lineal descendant of Abraham Lincoln, nor even whether he was of the same stock.

It is probable, however, that he was a lineal descendant of the great President.

The American people had come to acquiesce, more or less, in the law of heredity in the matter of public office. Thus John Adams had as a successor in the Presidency his son, and William Henry Harrison, his grandson. A son of Abraham Lincoln was, as early as 1896, a prominent candidate for the Presidency, and had already been sent as Minister to England.

In the twentieth century the negro vote had become the most powerful factor in elections. It held the balance of power, and both parties were compelled to court its support. Nothing was more natural than that a descendant of Abraham Lincoln, whom the negroes, out of that tendency to "hero-worship" of which I have spoken, were disposed to look upon as their "Moses," should be chosen as an available candidate by one of the great political parties. And to add to the strength of the appeal to this vote the "Emancipation Proclamation" was devised, and ascribed to the ancestor of the candidate.

The story was told to a people predisposed to accept it, and they did accept it without question. It accorded with their almost idolatrous veneration for the hero of the Civil War, which had led, in some way, to the enfranchisement of their race.

The story was a masterpiece of

political strategy, and was completely successful.

The descendant of Abraham Lincoln was triumphantly elected President of the United States.

History informs us that forgeries of this kind were not uncommon in former ages.

Thus, in the Presidential campaign of 1880 a letter appeared in the public press, a few weeks before the election, purporting to have been written by the Republican candidate, General Garfield, to a man named Morey, expressing views as to Chinese immigration which were extremely distasteful to the people of the Pacific States. The letter was a forgery ; but it was so successful that, before it was exposed, it served the purpose of turning the vote of California to Garfield's opponent.

Again there was in England the case of the forged letters of the great Irish patriot, Charles Stewart Parnell, which the London *Times* bought from a scoundrel named Pigott, and to which it gave the widest publicity.

It is not necessary to speak farther of this forgery, for my readers are, of course, familiar with it through the graphic pages of Gaboon's "Decline and Fall of the British Empire."

The famous "Forged Decretals" may also be cited. Originating in Spain, in the ninth century, they were only finally shown to be false in the fifteenth. The

reason for this is they contained nothing which was not in accord with
general belief, and so found ready
credence.

All this goes to show how readily,
with the favorable conditions existing in
the twentieth century, the Myth of the
Emancipation Proclamation could be
invented, and palmed off as genuine
history upon popular belief.

It is hardly necessary, I suppose, to
point out the inference to be drawn from
this discussion. The value of the
theories just stated is by no means to
be measured by their truth. It would
not impair their value if criticism still
higher than our present " higher criticism " should, in the future, supersede

them all by some theory still more "imaginative."

As said by Huxley, "he would be a rash man who should assert that any solution of these problems, as yet formulated, is exhaustive." *

The problem is to wipe out the old tradition, and it does not make much matter how this is done. The fertility of the new Timbuctoo school in brilliant theories, "half scientific, half imaginative," leads us to hope that, even if none of those thus far devised will "hold water," yet, in some future age, one may be constructed which will be altogether acceptable.

In the meantime, and until the dawn

* "Essays," p. 322.

of that millennium, and until all the possibilities of unheard and unheard of theories shall have been exhausted, the agnostic is entitled to insist upon a " suspension of judgment."

THE END.